MANAGEMENT
MADE EASY

Business Wisdom Series

MANAGEMENT
MADE EASY

Simple guidelines,
tips and tools
to make you a more
effective manager

S T E V E   H O L T

To order additional copies of this book, contact:
Xlibris
800-056-3182
www.Xlibrispublishing.co.uk
Orders@Xlibrispublishing.co.uk
721236

CONTENTS

Dedication

To my wonderful wife, Rita, without whose support I could not have written this.

Special thanks to my sons, Matthew and Ellis, and stepson, Nick, for reading the draft and being honest.

Acknowledgements

My acknowledgements go to all those I have worked with as a peer, subordinate and as a boss, either directly or indirectly. Also to those I have coached and mentored, who have given me frank and honest feedback that has enabled me to develop and grow into a better manager. Training courses and books are great (especially those you can read in a day), but it's the people that matter and it's their response that means the most.

I have two people in particular, Gary Steele and Russell Ingoe, with whom I have worked as both manager and colleague and that have helped me to become an improved manager. Their candid feedback whenI got it wrong and thanks when I got it right, have been instrumental in enabling me to write this book.

About the Author

Steve Holt graduated with an engineering degree from Middlesex University in 1979. His first jobs encompassed design, development, and manufacturing in the areas of domestic meters, micrographics, and FMCG. He moved into supply chain management in the late 1980s and has held numerous senior positions in multinational organisations.

Steve has developed extensive skills in business improvement, negotiation, supply-chain optimisation, and people management. Linking the process and the people to gain seamless change, management has become one of his greatest skills.

Much of Steve's success has come from on-the-job experience, and he openly admits that his mistakes have been his greatest learning.

He has managed people and processes around the globe, and this international experience has enabled him to develop an ability to work across many cultures.

He now runs his own consultancy, helping small to medium-sized businesses to benefit from his global experience.

'Having worked and lived in several countries around the world, Steve's insights provide great ways to navigate and excel in a variety of work environments and cultures' – VP, Marketing, at Wise Foods, Inc.

'Steve is one of the most approachable leaders I have worked with. He was always willing to knowledge share in a professor like fashion that was appreciated by all. His keen wit combined with sheer authenticity was always refreshing and left a significant impact on me' – Senior national account executive, Global Coffee Company.

The 'Made Easy' Cat

The cat can be seen as a symbol of both independence and friendship. In our business and personal lives, we need to find a balance between both, which the cat appears to achieve with unerring ease. The 'Made Easy' Cat is the constant across the '. . . Made Easy' range of books.

Follow the cat . . .

Preface

With over twenty years of management experience across many business and social levels, I have often made reference to books for guidance and support. I have perused many so-called management textbooks across the years, but the number I have read from cover to cover have amassed to maybe six, with the longest having some 150 pages. As a manager, I am looking for straightforward, easy elements that will steer and guide me and that I can interpret to suit my own behaviours and management style.

I recently saw a journal article that read 'People management is a simple equation'. Management has no formula or, in my mind, it shouldn't have! I find it disappointing when I read articles about management that say $x + y - z =$ result.

Everyone is different; even the most structured of people may act and behave differently under differing scenarios. When every element of any equation you may wish to conjure up is a variable, there cannot be an 'equals sign' in it! I have been privileged, over the years, to have worked with, for, and managed some great people, all of whom have taught me much. I have made many mistakes and hope that I have learnt from most of them. Some of my most significant learning has come from managing my people and the feedback they have given me.

I have written this from my own experiences and tried to give guide points for you to use as you see fit to suit your own style and methodology.

There are no formulae, no right and wrong answers, and a lot of what I have done has been through 'gut feel'. But, there are some processes which I truly believe are the foundation upon which a good manager can build. We all need to know our boundaries, and these can be defined within the processes outlined in the book.

Management is just one element, but a very large one, in ensuring that people are engaged and motivated in everything they do. In the business context, we often hear the saying, 'Our people are our greatest asset,' and yet more focus is put on other financial based assets than our people.

I have received many accolades across the years for my managerial skills, with many managers asking me for assistance and guidance. My most precious compliments were the tears and the upset shown when I announced my early retirement after twenty-six years with a particular corporation.

I write this book from an experiential perspective, having lived the ups and downs of being in a managerial position and look at it as an aid that I wish I'd had when I started out on my journey. There are some other great reads out there, which I will refer to throughout this book.

I am glad that you have the mindset to want to be a better manager. Please read on and take whatever you can from the following chapters to help you on your way through the business continuum we call management.

From Cocky Upstart to Frightened Manager!

Having graduated as a mechanical engineer, I spent the first two years of my working life in a high-volume manufacturing company as a process planning engineer. The company had a progressive approach to development and gave me opportunities to work across many disciplines such as plastics moulding, sheet metal fabrication, processing and plating, and maintenance and fitting. An excellent grounding for a greenhorn graduate!

Prospects were limited, and I took up a more project-based job with a company making micrographic and copying equipment. After a couple more years and a wife and young family, an opportunity came up to join a multinational organisation as a project manager. Bang – straight into line management. No experience, no training, no idea!

I now had four people who were depending on me to support their personal development aspirations. I was a confident, and sometimes cocky, self-centred, know-it-all, so what was the big deal anyway?

What a ridiculous attitude!

I was on a path of being friendly with my team without understanding how to treat them, earn their respect, and help them to grow. The 'sit up and take stock' moment was at the end of the year when the company appraisals and reviews were held.

These were discussed as a management group, and I felt totally inadequate and ill-prepared when, as a whole, the group agreed that one of my team was to be rated as below standard. I hadn't led the individual to believe that at all.

That was one of the hardest jobs I ever had to do as a manager. I have given many below-standard reviews across the years and even managed people out of the business, all of which have been easier than that first one and why? Simply because I didn't understand the fundamentals of management!

Following my disastrous start, I decided that I would find out if I could become a good manager and worked on understanding myself, other people, and environments to ensure that I got the best from a business's most important asset, its people.

Enjoy being a manager as one of a team, the leader but not always the decision maker. Embrace all it brings and learn something new every day.

Engineer or Manager?

This popular story illustrates a paradigm perception. I'm not certain of the origin of this tale, but you can find it in many places on the Internet.

A woman in a hot air balloon realised she was lost. She reduced altitude and spotted a man below. She descended a bit more and shouted:

'Excuse me, can you help me? I promised a friend I would meet him an hour ago, but I don't know where I am.'

The man below replied, 'You're in a hot air balloon, hovering approximately thirty feet above the ground. You're between forty and forty-one degrees north latitude and between fifty-nine and sixty degrees west longitude.'

'You must be an engineer,' said the balloonist.

'I am,' replied the man, 'how did you know?'

'Well,' answered the balloonist, 'everything you have told me is probably technically correct, but I've no idea what to make of your information, and the fact is, I'm still lost. Frankly, you've not been much help at all. If anything, you've delayed my trip by your talk.

'The man below responded, 'You must be in management.'

'I am,' replied the balloonist, 'but how did you know?'

'Well,' said the man, 'you don't know where you are or where you're going. You have risen to where you are due to a large quantity of hot air. You made a promise, which you've no idea how to keep, and you expect people beneath you to solve your problems. The fact is, you are in exactly the same position you were in before we met, but now, somehow, it's my fault.'

This story sums up the feelings of many people who are not in a management or supervisory role and at times has a ring of truth about it. There is a stigma, an 'us-and-them' consideration when the word 'manager' is uttered. All managers tend to be tarred with the same brush of 'management'. 'If management only knew what we did, everything would be all right.' Management sit in their ivory tower without a clue as to what the real world is like. Sweeping generalisations are based on a lack of knowledge and understanding and, in some cases, fear of the unknown. Ask many of the people who make these statements if they would like to be a manager, and in the main, they'd answer no. However, a business hierarchy needs management levels and so many of us take these positions which give us more responsibility, money, and, often, power over both people and other business assets. Across all walks of life, we have seen people abusing positions of power, and as such, we as managers need to be acutely aware of how our power affects both ourselves and those who work for and around us.

Taking up a management position is a conscious decision we take.

So why have I seen many examples where management positions have been filled with totally inappropriate people?

One issue is that it is often the only way to secure an increase in pay, and therefore, through either tenure of service or technical capability, you find yourself managing others.

I have an example of this which may ring true with some of you.

4

A thirty-something software engineer had developed products for a range of equipment, which were simply outstanding. His skills were without question, and he was a great asset to the business.

He was approached by another company and was offered more money for a similar job. Unfortunately, due to the structure of his current business, he was already at the top of his pay scale. The company didn't want to lose him, but the only way to increase his money was to promote him.

This promotion came with a new job specification, requiring him to manage three other people. Despite being given some management training, he continued to develop excellent products but failed to develop his team or ensure that the department was performing to the required standard and objectives.

At the end of just over a year, the individual was appraised as a manager. His previous technical excellence was somehow forgotten, and he eventually left the business. The moral here is that we're not all cut out to be managers and so many of us are doomed to be failures. It's not always our fault.

We all strive for more, and in the main, organisations are set up where the only way to increase income is through promotion. This is something of a recipe for failure. In their book, *The Peter Principle*,[1] Laurence Peter and Raymond Hull explain how 'in a hierarchy, every employee tends to rise to their level of incompetence'.

We mainly hear of the failures which stigmatise a position or role, but many people go on to become very good managers, and those of us who wish to pursue this should be given every opportunity to fulfil this desire. It's down to us to push back on stereotypes and change thinking.

5

Management or Managing Made Easy

'Wow, I've just been promoted to a manager. What do I do now?'

The word 'manager' fills us all with excitement, but it also brings with it a heck of a lot of responsibility. Anyone who takes this lightly or feels that it is a God-given right to own the title will surely come unstuck — eventually. Having been given the label, you immediately become 'management' and suddenly a void appears between you and the people you used to work with. This may not be evident immediately, with all the congratulations you will receive. Eventually, however, you will be bracketed along with all those people you used to talk about over lunch or in the pub after work, who apparently don't have a clue what they're talking about or how to do the job.

We all know this is ridiculous, and you have just been promoted because you are probably good at the job you do.

So why do the words 'manager' and 'management' often hold negative connotations? There are many and varied reasons for this, with the following list highlighting just a few.

- We don't understand what management really is even in its broadest terms.
- We don't understand the responsibility that comes with being a manager.

- We pay lip service to the needs of being a manager.
- We don't differentiate between process and people management.
- We appear to lose the sense of hearing when we get the title manager.
- We start to align ourselves with other managers.
- We believe that we are suddenly responsible for and capable of making all those decisions that others made for us before we got the title.
- We still look for what people are doing wrong, but now it's the others and not the managers.
- We become conceited and self-centred, with little regard for others.

I'm not suggesting that all managers respond in the same way or that all the above are prevalent in everyone, but this is what others see. There are also times when it is right and correct to be self-centred, when telling, rather than listening, is the only option, but it is a good manager who knows which cards to play and when.

Managers who are able to bridge that hypothetical gap with non-managers whilst keeping sacred their managerial status will build high performing, trusting teams and earn respect from those who are above and below them in the company's hierarchy.

Many of the behaviours shown in the list above can be combated through greater levels of empathy across the whole business structure and understanding how to behave and react in certain situations. That is the skill-based elements of management and will be discussed in more detail later in the book. Now then, the differentiation of people and process is one that has frustrated me throughout my many years as a manager and my working across different cultures.

We are all aware that each person is different in every aspect of work and social life. A myriad psychologists have written papers, documents, and books, run courses, and given lectures, which categorise who we are, how we work and behave, how we interact with others, and what our preferences for learning and working are.

When you undergo one of these profiling techniques and you have completed your questionnaire, you are compartmentalised. We, and the others privy to the information, agree that this is who and what we are, and we are immediately labelled, both by ourselves and others.

I'm not suggesting that these processes are wrong, just hoping that people treat them with respect for what they are as guides to understanding and not definitive character categorisations.

I have known HR departments to allocate a particular profile to specific jobs. Not attaining a 100 per cent fit to the profile will result in them not getting to interview. How crazy is that to say that we're no good based on how we filled in a questionnaire?

A core management skill is to understand how different people behave and like to be treated so that we can optimise the performance of and relationship with that individual. Treating people like people is fundamental to getting the best out of them.

Let's have a closer look now at the people versus process elements of management.

The personal profiling and greater in-depth understanding of an individual is key to developing strong bonds, giving the manager the freedom to direct and guide with willing participants. Why then, as managers, do we hide behind the process of our job function and use that as our tool for managing people? I believe that it is because many of us are frightened of the consequences of the relationship and feel vulnerable when talking about feelings.

Will I be taken advantage of and lose control if I develop a more open interaction between myself and my employees?

Let us not forget that our employees are the greatest asset we have, and in order to get optimum performance from this asset, we need to understand and manage each one individually. Managing through process, whilst getting things done, will not necessarily deliver optimised performance.

Let's now look at what we really need to be doing to get the best from our people.

It's OK to be Friendly – Even Friends

The fine balance between being a 'mate' with your subordinates or a distant misanthrope is not easily taught or adopted. It is fair to say that it comes easier to some than others, and if you find it hard, then it is a must that you seek help to either be tougher at one end of the spectrum or more open and accepting at the other.

As alluded to earlier, I was the friendly sort who caught a cold and had to learn to be tougher and separate friendship from business relationships. It's not easy and that first discussion with a subordinate will be really difficult for both. At the end of the day, you are going to be measured on your results, which include your people's results as well.

So what did I do?

Following the debacle of the year-end appraisal, I was not in a good place with my team. I had to clawback any semblance of respect that may have been there previously in order to become a more effective boss. I initially sought help and advice from a sagely manager whom I held in high esteem. We had socialised together, and yet in the work environment, he commanded respect, and his rapport with subordinates was excellent. The advice was simple:

'Don't try to be something you're not. Stay true to yourself.'

'You can be crystal clear about what is needed in a friendly way. You don't have to be standoffish to be in control.'

'Admit your mistakes and set yourself new personal goals to get to where you want.'

'Share your goals with your people. It may sound strange, but they know you're the boss and with it come responsibilities and pressures that they probably don't want or need. You'll be surprised how much they'll help you.'

'Where appropriate, explain the rationale behind your decisions, especially those which may appear unpopular.'

The first thing I did was to establish in my own mind where I was and where I wanted to be. I have always been a very sociable person, so to become remote was not an option. I did, however, need to change behaviours.

I succeeded on my personal goals for the next three months, which I thought would create the right environment within the team and establish a greater level of trust in me being able to hit targets. I ate a little humble pie with the individual who had received a poor appraisal, and we spent some time going over what he had actually done versus the expectation of the business as a whole. It came to light that he was not surprised at the decision reached but more upset that he had no forewarning of the pending outcome.

This is a really important point to bring out. People don't like surprises. If something is not going in the right direction, nip it in the bud immediately and set a new course.

It's also good to be aware that your subordinates will talk to each other about nearly everything, so the discussions I had were soon public knowledge within the group. If you want anything to remain confidential, make sure you say so at the time of the discussion. Anyway, as I'd been open and honest, things progressed extremely well. A little humility can go a long way to gaining support and developing more robust relationships.

As the years rolled on, this method of management became more and more natural, and consequently, I have had some great friendships with people who worked for me. The key is to set the ground rules for the day job so that there are no misunderstandings. You will read later the importance of having robust objectives that steer and guide the working relationship; these will enable you to establish the ground rules and will be the basis for keeping work and friendships separate.

I have never had to dismiss a subordinate who had become a friend, but I believe that although it would be hard, with sound objectives or other just cause, it would not be too difficult.

It's really difficult to differentiate between being one of the team and being the boss. If you can master this and create a balance in your approach, then you will have conquered one of the biggest management challenges. I'll demonstrate this by giving two examples of managers I have worked with across the years.

Manager A runs a finance department with approximately ten clerks. The one thing I remember about this department is the enormous void between the manager and the staff. The department was not quite the 'toxic energy dump' referred to in Lundin, Paul, and Christensen's book *Fish*,[3] but not far off.

To illustrate the issue, I will use the example of a doctor's appointment. Whilst I accept that we should all try to make our appointments outside work hours, it is not always possible to do so. This scenario was not isolated to this particular manager.

The business day runs from 0845 to 1645 with a thirty-minute lunch break. There was some flexibility in the actual time of this break and so people would arrange appointments within this window. For fire purposes, it is necessary to sign in and out every time you come into and leave the building. The employees dutifully signed in and out whenever they went out for an appointment.

Manager A would use this signed fire register as a time-keeping record and demand that the employees made up any time over the half hour allocated for lunch. Quite within their rights, and you may think it to be understandable.

What do you think the response of the employees was when at the end of a month, when the focus and pressure came on the finance department to release the figures and there was a need for a few extra minutes to be worked to ensure they came out on time? Most requests for 'Can you stay a little longer to finish this off?' were met with a no.

Manager B was a production manager whose production lines ran from 0800 to 1800, with a sixty-minute lunch break. Once again, employees would use this hour to slip out to town for a few things as this could be easily achieved due to the proximity of the shops.

If the employees were a few minutes late, it wasn't really an issue as the manager would probably use this time to get closer to his staff and keep his hand in by filling in on the production line until the employee returned. It was always only a couple of minutes or so, and the manager enjoyed this little bit of hands-on.

What do you think happened when there was a need to quickly increase output, and the manager asked for volunteers to work on a little longer?

With this manager being so flexible and friendly to his staff, covering their extra minutes, you'd have thought that they would be only too willing to reciprocate.

Well, they weren't! This manager was seen as soft and so he had no control or influence over his work force.

To be an effective manager and remain close to your people, you need to set what I will call 'flexible constraints'. Allow your people that little bit of flexibility and don't be over zealous with the constraints.

The use of subliminal control is very effective. If someone returns late from lunch by a few minutes, then once they have settled back in to their work, go over and ask 'Was everything OK at lunchtime?' You'll probably get a positive response, but what you will have done is registered in their mind that you are well aware of what happened. If this flexibility is abused, then you have the right to impose total constraint.

Steve's top tips:

- Be consistent
- No surprises
- Flexible constraints

Management by Objectives (MBO) or Is It MBF?

Managing through the use of objectives is a great way to ensure that progress discussions with your employees are always meaningful and focussed.

Be sure that at the start of every year and at regular intervals throughout the year, you review and agree on the results achieved against the objectives set. Highlight any gaps against the targets (e.g. sales targets, production output, successful recruitments, etc.), and re-confirm the objectives from now until the next review. Don't do what so many managers do, and use the objectives as a way to tell your people what they're doing wrong. So many inexperienced or inept managers don't review on a regular basis because they haven't set the time aside in their diaries ; they are frightened for their own jobs and/or they just don't like talking to people.

This is what turns MBO into MBF – Management By Fear.

The review time should be a reasonably relaxed affair for both parties and a time when you can both talk about the great things achieved and how you're going to build on them over the coming months. This meeting should never be the first time you bring up a problem, be it performance related or disciplinary, with your employee. Any issues identified in the interim period must be tackled immediately and a process established for resolution. We will discuss this in more detail later.

As a species, however, we do have a tendency to focus on the negative aspects of a situation or condition. If, for instance, you ask someone how they are feeling, they are more likely to tell you about an ailment or a pending issue, irrespective of their current state of health. Ask someone to comment on a sport or artistic performance, and you will invariably hear about what was bad about it and not the good. If you are ever in the situation where you have to get feedback from other people, ask them for at least three positive things before a negative statement is made. I think you'll be surprised at how many people will struggle to get three.

From a managerial perspective, what is wrong with both catching people doing things right and also doing things wrong? Blanchard and Johnson in their book, *The One Minute Manager*[2] talk about 'one-minute praisings' with the mantra of 'help people reach their full potential — catch them doing something right.' How good do you feel when someone says 'well done' or 'great job'? Your subordinates' feelings are no different than yours. They are not inferior to you because they are subordinate; in fact, you may find out that many are more intelligent than you. If you treat them like human beings and reward when reward is the right thing to do, they will not only be more motivated, they will help you achieve your goals. In addition, they will be more accepting of constructive criticism and reprimands when required. Blanchard and Johnson also talk about 'one-minute reprimands'.

The above is easy to write and say, but is it easy to do?

We have our own job to do as well as manage others and so sitting with them and agreeing objectives takes time — which I don't have!

Reviewing their objectives, say every quarter, takes time — which I don't have.

Appraising their performance at the end of each year takes time — which I don't have.

If this is you, then what I have to say is, 'If you want to be a manager and be paid as a manager, then manage your time and do the job correctly.' How often do you hear the phrase 'I don't have the time'?

I put it to you that time is a perceived barrier made up to suit our own needs to put things off. If we look at the productive element of our day, I would suggest that the majority of us are paid for more hours than we actually work! The meetings and discussions around the coffee machine are important, but we can easily sacrifice one of these to give each of our people a more formal hour each month or quarter as necessary. The informal discussions and interactions, which were covered in greater detail in the chapter 'It's OK to Be Friendly – Even Friends', are equally as important and are a vital piece of the whole management pie. Here, however, we are looking specifically at MBO, so let's focus on the next phase of setting the objectives.

Setting Objectives

What a great way to start a management-subordinate relationship, sitting down and discussing what you both want to achieve! So why don't we do it more often? Maybe, from a managerial perspective, it's a way to have a hold over our subordinates if we don't tell them everything and from the subordinates' point of view, a way to get away with things that were never discussed.

What a way to run a business relationship, well, any relationship when you come to think about it!

So how do we set about creating a set of objectives that are acceptable to both parties, are meaningful, and yet stretching ? I use the last word advisedly, as sometimes we just want something done that is neither difficult nor brain teasing. However, in the main, as managers, we should want to develop our people in order that they may grow as the business grows, keep abreast of new technologies, and progress towards promotion if so required.

Wow, I have seen some humdingers of objectives from the sublime *achieve sales targets* to the — whatever you want to call this — *325 boxes shipped by 4.30 p.m. each and every day of the week from Monday through Friday. Collection by national carrier to be between the hours of 4 p.m. and 4.30 p.m. Any shortfall of the 325 boxes will be caught up the following day. Any shortfall from 1,625 by 4.30 p.m. of each Friday will be charged at 50p per box not shipped and deducted equally from each employee's wages working in the department.*

In the first example, how can we as managers have our finger on the pulse of what's happening and then have a meaningful discussion over three words? These can be referred to as DOGIs or Declarations Of Good Intent. The second example is very specific, very measurable, maybe achievable, definitely time-bounded, but not necessarily realistic. It fits all but one of the key elements for setting objectives, plus it has a facet which is both punitive and demotivational.

How do we set proper objectives?

Let's be SMART about this. This acronym has been around for a long time and yet we often fail to use it effectively to either develop new objectives or review and check existing ones. SMART stands for:

Specific
Measurable
Achievable
Realistic
Time-bound

Specific — exactly what it says on the tin, be specific about what is to be achieved.

Not 'achieve sales targets' but

a. to hit at least 85 per cent of agreed quarterly sales targets in each sector.
b. to produce up to 15,000 packets of oat cereal every day, depending on sales requirements.
c. to ship between 300 and 325 packets each day.

Measurable — there must be something that can be measured so that all parties know when they have either hit or missed the objective.

a. Quarterly sales targets are for 1,000 units each quarter in all sales areas.
b. Over three shifts in twenty-four hours, each shift shall be capable of producing 6,500 packets of oat cereal, with a minimum capacity of 5,000 units.
c. 300 – 325 packets to be available for collection each day by 4.30 p.m.

Achievable — this one often catches people. It is important to set targets that will stretch the individual(s) get the grey matter working and maybe create a little intrigue or challenge. However, not too stretching as to be impractical. For example, you can't ask a sales person to make ten visits in five different countries where his responsibility covers all of Western Europe.

Only you and the person you are having the conversation with can say if the objectives are truly achievable. As a subordinate, the tendency will be to set the objectives on the light side to overachieve. As a manager, it is our job to make sure that the objectives are set at a reasonable level to ensure that the individual or team are stretched to their optimum capability/capacity.

Once this discussion has been had, you must then ensure that they are-

Realistic — another difficult discussion, since one man's realism isn't always the same as another's. In the example above regarding the shipping of boxes, you can see that 325 boxes each day by 4.30 p.m. may be achievable but may not be realistic. A shipping department can be influenced by many factors outside of its control, for example, production, supplies, couriers, sales, and others.

It is therefore important to ensure that these types of elements are considered. If a salesperson typically has to drive fifty miles between customers across city centres, then this must be taken into account. I'm not suggesting that one should be soft, but as the element says, be realistic.

Time bound — take a look at your own objectives or the one's you've set with your employees or even some of your larger business objectives and count how many of them have a reference to time.

If the objectives are not time-bound, we can never praise or reprimand for attaining or missing them. The scenario of the boxes is a great example of an objective being time-bound.

By 4.30 p.m. each and every day of the week from Monday through Friday. Collection by national carrier to be between the hours of 4 p.m. and 4.30 p.m.

However, most of us will be working on longer term projects with less specific times and dates. It is still important to time-bound them. Whatever we are working on, there will be a deliverable that is expected by a certain time, so agree to it and write it down.

First draft of the proposal completed by 23rd March. Final document to be completed by 31st May; all quality audits to be completed for HR by the end of quarter one.

These are just examples of what a time-bound element of an objective may look like.

Let's look at a couple of good examples for a complete objective.

We will achieve a cost saving of 3 per cent on the purchase of cardboard cartons against last year's purchase price when the contract is renewed in quarter 2 of next year.

Production efficiency will improve by two percentage points to attain a minimum of 99 per cent on time and in full delivery to warehouse as detailed in the production plan.

Having set our SMART objectives, can we sit back and just wait for our people to deliver, or do we need to do other things?

Setting objectives is just the start to becoming a manager. We need to do a lot more in order to help our people achieve these objectives.

We also need to manage the performance.

Steve's top tips

- Regular reviews
- SMART objectives

Helping Your People Succeed
(Performance Management)

So we've got the hang of this MBO stuff as all our objectives are SMART, and no one is in any doubt of what we are trying to achieve. Now we have to help them achieve it.

We've employed people to do the job and that's what they're paid for! I know that it's not your job to do their job for them, but without some help and guidance, and since their objectives will reflect yours, you may not succeed. A little helpful input, in the form of reviews and discussions, regarding performance will go a long way to helping you become a better manager.

We talked in the previous chapter about objectives and the examples were very much focussed on tasks. It is, however, important to ensure that some personal development objectives are set. These may be in the area of attitude, time-keeping, follow-through, communication, report writing, setting own objectives, or any similar topics that you as a manager feel are important for the individual's growth.

It is important at this stage to say that you need to gain agreement from the individual that they concur with these development-need areas. If they don't, then you will need to approach them with facts and feedback, possibly from others that highlight this need.

Once again, we're not into the realms of developing nuclear physics, we're talking about people and with this comes a plethora of different attitudes, needs, and wants. Throughout this book, you will notice that I make reference to sitting down with and talking to your people on a regular basis. It has always amazed me how alien this appears to so many managers and yet it is what they want or even demand from their own scalar chain.

Performance appraisal is more often than not considered as the big stick at the end of the year that provides an excuse as to why you should not get a performance-related pay increase.

My manager and his colleagues will be looking at where I have failed and use this against me.

If we want to get better at a sport, then we go out and practise on a regular basis. If we are coaching someone in a sport, we would work with them on a few new areas for improvement, let them go away and practise, and follow up at an agreed time in the near future. Why, oh why when there is a performance-management process in place, do we so often leave it for a whole year before we talk to our people about their performance?

The process is simple; it is us as managers who complicate it by not giving the necessary time. The longer we put off our reviews, the longer the reviews take. So here's how I would suggest that the process is set out:

- After you have established your own and your departmental objectives, meet as soon as possible with your employees.
- Outline where you'd like the department to go and get some feedback from the employees on these objectives. Change them if necessary and/or if possible to ensure buy-in from the employees.
- Set the individual's business objectives. This is a discussive and iterative process.
- Establish the short, medium and longer term goals to be achieved throughout the appraisal timeline.

- Establish and agree review dates and times. I would suggest a minimum of three within a one-year period.
- Get the employee to express areas of personal development.
- Outline areas where you would like to see the employee grow and improve, if not already raised by themselves.
- Agree on the areas of focus and set out the process for review and any help or support the individual may need, e.g. coaching, training courses, buy and read the *Management Made Easy* book!
- Set out review dates and times. These may differ from the business objectives review. That is up to you.
- Put the review dates in your diary and make them a priority. Change only when absolutely necessary. Another meeting is not an excuse to change a review date and time.

When and if you see your employee(s) achieving an objective (be it business or personal) outside the review times, congratulate them, buy them a coffee, and pat them on the back. You can always congratulate them again at the review.

This leads on nicely for us to look at what to do if your employees are not achieving either their personal or business objectives.

I have had the privilege of being asked to coach and mentor a number of people over my career. More often than not, the areas for development have been in the behavioural, managerial, and personal development arena. When I ask a question like 'What would you change?', the response invariably relates to their manager not picking up on issues and letting them go on for far too long. If you don't tell people that they're heading in the wrong direction, how will they know?

In the 'Management by Objectives' chapter and the previous paragraph, we touched on the point about catching people doing things right and making them feel good.

Acting in the moment!

It is just as, if not more important to catch things early when they are going off track. We all know this, so why don't we do it? The longer we leave something, the more difficult it is to recover the situation.

There is also the impact seen by others where the failure to meet a business objective has an effect on another department.

Your management may also come into question if one of your subordinates fails to hit a deadline. It's surprising how much help you can get when others are impacted!

You've bothered setting personal and development objectives with your employee(s), so if you see them veering off track, help them. Don't let them aimlessly go down the wrong path only to be chastised at a later date. Who benefits from that type of management action? Neither the subordinate nor you. Because these examples are often more personal, we find it hard to address them. This is why objectives and regular performance reviews are so important.

Stop reading now for a second and use the margin to write yourself a note to discuss and set some performance targets and review dates with your employees.

OK, done that? Good. Carry on now with Managing the Review Process.

Managing the Review Process

You will have established by now that, I firmly believe that, the review process should be considered a key management tool and incorporated into everyone's portfolio. However, the process can fall into disrepute if it is not managed and handled correctly. Abuse of the process is the one thing that causes more pain and grief than anything else.

Let me outline a few dos and don'ts for running the process.

Do

- fix the date and time in your diary.
- book a venue. Don't leave it to chance that you can find a meeting room and don't hold the discussion in reception. These discussions form the basis of an employee's future, so you owe it to them to be organised.
- take in notes and specific examples of both good and improvement areas. Throughout the time between reviews, it's OK to keep notes on your employees. This way, you can be specific, enabling both of you to discuss around an event. It is particularly important for corrective elements as opposed to praise. Here's an example:

> Manager: I don't think you handled the software interface discussion very well.
>
> Employee: Oh, in what way?
>
> Manager: Ur, um well, you need to be a bit more considerate.
>
> Employee: In what way?
>
> Manager: I just heard you didn't handle it well. That's all. You need to be a bit more considerate.

This employee has no idea what he or she has done, either right or wrong, and has no clue as to how to change and/or improve. People will change behaviours if you can be specific in your feedback.

- allow enough time for the discussions. Having to cut a review short because you didn't book the room for long enough is one of the most frustrating elements in the process. It can also give an impression of reducing the worth to your employee.
- turn your phone off and give the employee your full attention.
- agree that it's OK to make notes and share them at the end.
- accept responsibility for the feedback given. It's you giving the feedback. You have to own it and feed it back in your own way even if it is an example from someone else (see below for deferred responsibility).
- ensure that the employee is the main focus. It's their review, not yours.

Don't

- cancel the meeting unless you really have to.
- rush through the difficult stuff. This is usually the feedback that is most valuable to the employee as it is where he or she can make changes for improvement. It's normally an area where we as managers are most uncomfortable, so moving swiftly away makes us feel better.
- defer responsibility for feedback. This to me is one of the biggest no-nos in managing. 'Jimmy, you're not doing a bad job, but over there in accounts, they think you're too abrupt. I personally don't have a problem with this but see what you can do, OK?' If you don't have a problem with it, then support Jimmy with the accounts people. If they've convinced you that there is an issue, however minor, then you have to own it as well and feed it back as yours. 'I've had some feedback from accounts, Jimmy, about you being a little abrupt. The examples they have given me are . . .

You're not like it with me, so let's discuss what's going on and work on improving our relationship with them.'

- hide behind the system. 'Listen, Beryl, let's get this over and done with quickly. I know neither of us like this appraisal process, but HR say that we've got to do it. I know we'd both prefer to be getting on with the job. What do you say?' Just think about what message you're giving here.

Steve's top tips:

- Be focused on both task and personal development.
- Be specific with examples.
- Allow time for reviews – regular and often.
- It's all about their development, not yours.

The Day-to-Day Process

You now have all these tools to create a fairly formal management process, but on a day-to-day basis, the interaction between you and your people is likely to be a balance between the formal and the informal.

How are you going to handle that?

Be yourself, don't try to change any of your fundamental values or you'll be seen as being false. The facets that you can change are your behaviours.

The discussions between you and your subordinates that have taken place while you were developing and setting direction and objectives should have helped you to understand each of the individuals a little more. It's not going to be 'a one size fits all' approach when dealing with them as you will need to adapt your behaviour and words to suit each individual. Some will want to take more initiative and respond to a 'go and try for yourself' approach. Others may not react immediately and work best when given time to reflect.

If you find it difficult to assess individuals and their needs, why not ask some of your peers who interact with them and agree on an appropriate approach? Whether your team is large or small, diverse or like-minded, some team building and/or assessment will always aid the overall dynamic. It's down to you as the manager what you choose from the full-on team building/outdoor activity to a couple of hours or a half-day 'get to know' each other with some simple assessment of how we all like to work, act, behave, and respond.

There are myriad processes which look at how an individual behaves, reacts, and likes to learn from IQ tests to neurolinguistic programming. I have found Gardner's Multiple Intelligencies[4] and the way it is described in Eric Jensen's book *Brain Based Learning*[5] a really useful tool in helping me better understand my people. You may find other tools useful for you.

In terms of creating a team or understanding a team's profile and why it is working or not carrying out what is commonly referred to as a 'Belbin assessment' is always useful. This is based on the work carried out by the British researcher Raymond Meredith Belbin[6] and published in his book, *Managing Teams*, in 1981. Belbin Team Roles are used to identify people's behavioural strengths and weaknesses in the workplace. Once you've got to grips with how people like to be treated, how they learn, and their individual behavioural traits, you'll find yourself dealing with people on a much more even footing and dealing with conflict in a calmer, more controlled way. As the manager, you will be able to formulate your arguments and discussion points in a way that gets through to each individual in the most effective way. Knowing their behavioural characteristics, their strengths, and their weaknesses will enable you to give direction that best suits them to drive the whole team to achieve its as well as your objectives.

Remember, everyone will make mistakes, it's inevitable. The strength of a great manager is how mistakes are managed, resolved, and corrections put in place to ensure non-reoccurrence. If the mistake is due to negligence, then you may need to take disciplinary action. However, most mistakes are simply that, mistakes, so as the manager, you must first of all accept that these will happen and then work practically with your subordinate towards the resolution.

Don't take over, coach, and guide them and let them do the work. This way, they will learn more and be less likely to repeat errors made. Once this has been done and the problem resolved, you can have the discussion as to what went wrong and what needs to happen to ensure that the problem doesn't come back. You may, at this point, raise any disappointment you may have, directly with the individual, on a one-to-one basis.

Never involve a third party unless it is a disciplinary issue. Also, always support your subordinate in discussion with other managers. Irrespective of what is said by others, when genuine mistakes happen, you will get far more reward from your team by supporting them than you will from your peers if you humiliate them.

As you develop your own methods for interfacing with both the individuals and the team, you will find yourself with more time to focus on your own tasks, having built up your confidence to let your team get on and do the things that you have agreed with them.

Don't forget, though, the fact that you've developed a team of people that can manage their own objectives doesn't preclude you from checking in, asking for progress reports, and keeping abreast of their work. This is what creates that sustainable and effective management process that allows individuals to succeed whilst being there for them as necessary and keeping them on their toes.

Steve's top tips:

- Be yourself. Change your behaviours, not values.
- Find out what makes your people tick.
- Don't be afraid to check up on progress.

- Let them get on with it and help them overcome hurdles.
- Accept mistakes are inevitable and work with them to solve.
- Support your people through mistakes, both internally and externally.

Now Get On and Do It

OK, you've read the written word, and you now have to translate it into tangible actions that will aid you in your endeavours. I have written this from the point of view of my own experiences. We are all different and act, behave, and feel different things.

Take the general process points and use them as and where you feel comfortable in your own way and in your own time. Being a good or even great manager will not happen overnight.

Do not attempt to implement everything at once, or you'll drown.

Try small elements and see how they go for you.

Use one or two individuals within your team to help you start (depends on where you are and the relationships you have with your people).

Share with them your desires for improvement and let them help you along the way by giving you feedback on the things that went well and the areas where they think you could improve.

What a great way to start on your management improvement journey!

My hope is that this book has given you a few hints and tips and a basis on which you can build to become one of our great managers.

Thanks for reading.

References

1. *The Peter Principle* (1969) by *Laurence J. Peter* and Raymond Hull. Souvenir Press Ltd; New Edition (23 August 1994).

2. *The One Minute Manager* (1982) by *Ken Blanchard* and Spencer Johnson. Harper; New Edition (1 September 2011).

3. *Fish* (2000) by Stephen C. Lundin Ph.D., Harry Paul, and John Christensen. Hodder (5 September 2002).

4. *The Theory of Multiple Intelligences* (1983) by Howard Gardner. Basic Books (31 March 1993).

3. *Brain Based Learning* (1996) by Eric Jensen. Corwin; Second Edition (12 August 2008).

4. *Managing Teams* (1981) by Raymond Meredith Belbin. A Butterworth-Heinemann Title; New Edition (11 March 1996).

The Business Wisdom Series

Management Made Easy is the first in this Business Wisdom series of books, with the next book being *Negotiation Made Easy*. Further books in this series will be available soon.

Lightning Source UK Ltd.
Milton Keynes UK
UKOW04f0615210116

266830UK00002B/130/P